Tanpura's
Strum

Tanpura's Strum

A Collection of Haiku, Tanka and Micropoems

By Jesal Kanani

GLOBAL
COLLECTIVE
PUBLISHERS

Published by Global Collective Publishers
2628 West Chester Pike, Suite 281
Broomall, Pennsylvania 19008, U.S.A.
www.globalcollectivepublishers.com

Copyright © Jesal Kanani, 2021
Print ISBN: 978-1-954021-32-7
eBook ISBN: 978-1-954021-33-4

For My Father

For All Women

Table of Contents

Preface   ix

Acknowledgements   xv

    I. Tanpura's Strum   1

   II. Of Kadipatta Leaves and Everything
       in Between   21

  III. Tell the Hairstylist,
       Keep It Long   52

   IV. First Day of Spring   75

    V. Moon Face   101

   VI. Corn Cobs at Kisama   117

  VII. His Body Is My Home   129

 VIII. Grow Wild Like Kelp   138

   IX. Small Talk in Office   156

    X. Moons of Different Planets   163

   XI. Embers of a Diwali Sparkler   177

XII. Of What We Used To Be   181

XIII. Words Become Play   200

Credit to the Illustrators   203

About the Cover Artist   204

Preface

Sometime in August 2013, after losing my father to cancer, I ended up in a writing workshop among the low hills of Karjat, seeking refuge in two things that gave me comfort: writing and nature. The sky was overcast. As we sat facing a large bay window that opened to a verdant plain in which a river gurgled unmindfully, the scenery was at odds with everything I was feeling inside. Only the sky reflected what I felt.

It was here a friend explained how he constructed haiku, "Take two images, place them side-by-side, such that the juxtaposition turns meaningful," and with that, I began my journey into poetry. He encouraged us to take a walk in the fields to snag ideas for our poems. In those days, most of my thoughts rested with my father and though the fields must've been filled by rain-tipped blades of grass and fringed by velvety hills, what came to my mind was this:

> black butterfly
> descend gently
> on young green leaves

If you must approach, Death, do it kindly.

I remember that despite the heartache there was a glimmer of gratification in that moment, for being able to express my feelings in a new poetic form.

But I didn't take to haiku just then, for I had many pages still to write about my father, and of a grief that was to be excoriated only through long journal entries.

❊ ❊ ❊

Before coming to haiku, I had written longform prose — short stories, essays. When an idea for a story lingered in my mind for days, I took it as a sign to begin writing, exploring. In this writing routine, the haiku then turned out to be a refreshing change. Hai-ku true to its name — the hai for amusement, lightness and the ku for verse — offered me the chance to respond to a range of stimuli with words and as I wrote in the rush of the moment, I grew delightfully aware, of a lingering lightness, no weight of words (characteristic of longform) to be carried forward to the next day. This, I found liberating.

Initial forays into haiku sensitised me to observe nature even more closely. There was comfort in the regularity of the day progressing, in watching the gradient of light change outside the window and the coolness of the moon come pouring in on to the terracotta tiles of the balcony, night after night. And arresting sights to behold: crystals of raindrops on a windowpane, an empty bottle belly dancing to the breeze, the many shades to a sunset. Somehow recording the evenness and oddness of these occurrences and drawing out their connections to life was calming at a time when my father's loss had made my footing in the world unsteady. Maybe I was trying to write myself into happiness.

I'd like to spend some time here, talking about haiku. Haiku usually relies on images to tell its story:

after lunch hour
the empty tables
reserved for sparrows

Do you see the two images, juxtaposed? The empty tables with the sparrows? When struck together like this, the images spark an entire scene: I see a languid day where the poet, lingers after lunch hour in a restaurant, evidently with more time on her hands than the busy sparrows she writes about; perhaps it is the weekend or maybe summer holidays, when the sparrows are out and about looking for food for their fledglings. Haiku, as a form, is replete with seasonal references.

❋ ❋ ❋

It was in April 2016, in a bookstore in Shinjuku, Tokyo, that I first came across tanka in Machi Tawara's book, Salad Anniversary. Holding it, was like bringing up a conch shell to my ear—it echoed of a long-lost familiarity.

That evening, standing in the bookstore, reading tanka after tanka, in someone else's journal, I was astonished with the sharing of secrets between lines, the intimacy of words that leapt out to me.

In its essence, tanka is a diary, a record keeping of sorts, of things and thoughts. It was a revelation then that words that would've marched into pages could be condensed in five phrases.

How does tanka do it?

Tanka, by digging its feet in the universality of humanness assumes a certain familiarity—maybe, you too must've felt what I did and so doesn't spend time in setting up stage. There is little embellishment, as it sing-songs its way into the experience of daily life. Sometimes a tanka is factually dated, like an entry of a diary, and even if not, it is invested in the present moment, in the now, and so, always explored, in present tense.

Like haiku, tanka is a visual poem, the difference being that tanka also travels into the landscape of emotions, with the image often working as a catalyst in drawing out an emotional response.

fourth of May (date)
holding a new life
in my arms (image)
ask myself stunned—
is she mine, is she mine? (emotional response)

Did you notice there is no careful build-up to this moment, nor a rush to end it; it is just a single moment, in all its entirety that the tanka dives into and resurfaces like a lotus blooming, amplifying the experience of having lived it?

A mother holding and gazing at her baby for the first time: in moments of extreme joy (or despair), doesn't one leap out of the world, out of oneself, scarcely believing if this at all, is happening!

It had been three years since I lost my father and after pages and pages written about him—which I couldn't bear to call memories for then he would be irretrievably gone— the edge of pain had finally dulled and other things had started appearing in my journal. Haunted by the thought that the grains of time were falling swiftly, that all of life was dated—in the subsequent scramble I wanted to freeze time and urgently record everything that was happening to me. And maybe that is why tanka resonated the way it did, that Spring evening faintly fragrant with cherry blossoms and possibilities.

As I ventured to write my tanka stories (for that is what tanka feels to me, a story clicked of a particular moment – external or internal), I felt it was large enough to accommodate all my feelings: the imaginative endings and beginnings my life would've taken and the what-ifs weaved their way in. I wrote poems that felt closest to my feelings, to my truth, sometimes even over tanka as it 'should be'. And yet, like playing in a courtyard I wasn't too worried about getting lost, because the framework of tanka—that of five phrases—was set.

Soon enough, what began as an autobiographical experiment cast its roots, like a banyan tree—far and wide—into the osmotic imagining of the experiences of others. The canvas for my wordbrush expanded with every drop of ink on paper.

Motherhood, heartbreak, loss, love—even the tangible: vegetables, beaches, forests and salons, oh, I wanted to write about it all! The brevity of form made it possible to cover a stunning range of landscapes—emotional and physical. Like a jigsaw puzzle, I kept arranging, rearranging lines in poems, addicted to that dose of serotonin that washed over me when a haiku or tanka set well.

When I find moments that rise up like iridescent bubbles through the rough tumble of a day, there's an expansion of my consciousness. And the world transforms into a place that waits longingly to be written about.

Jesal Kanani
Thane, India

Acknowledgements

The poems in this book, are an amalgamation of many people, places and things. While writing poetry, the people mentioned here have appeared in my mind at different times — often enough — that it would be safe to say, some of the atoms and molecules that make up this book, have been borrowed from them. Some of these extraordinary people are the reason why these words were written in the first place, others have been the wind beneath my fingers.

Having all of them come together on this page then is like throwing a house-party on paper, in pandemic times, where I get to celebrate their ways of being, the lights that they continue to be, even as they remain unselfconscious of this immutable fact: their actions alter the courses of people's lives.

With deep gratitude then to:

Raamesh Gowri Raghavan, for introducing me to haiku.

Maud Casey, at the University of Maryland, teacher extraordinaire, who showed us the sacred place from which to look into stories. And how to read another writer's work, offer feedback, no matter how different it maybe from the style one practises or is familiar with.

For making me see my words had heft.

The MFA program at University of Maryland, for supporting my education. For workshops that make fledgling writers believe their words are worthy of being read and discussed in class. My writing workshop classmates and friends — Erin Baggett and Amy Joust.

My teachers at the University of Maryland, for helping me see the arterial roads and alleyways in literature, for introducing me to so many fine writers and writing styles. For the importance of punctuation.

The Missouri Review for publishing my first story, for the thrill of seeing my work — in print, for the first time — reach out to fine readers.

Machi Tawara for writing Salad Anniversary. For showing that even a few phrases can hold within them so much of life, so much intimacy. For the freshness and joy that erupts in her work.

My English teachers in school – Mrs. Jaiswal, Mrs. Ghosh, Mrs. Subramaniam, Mrs. Chaturvedi for facilitating my love for English as a subject and a language.

My primary school library that housed so many books; my primary school librarian, Mrs. Ray, whose welcoming smile never dimmed, despite me walking in every single day, to exchange a book.

The team of brothers who ran the Reader's Corner, a library at the corner of my street, that required temple-like, one take off their shoes before entering in.

Mrs. Shobha Kelkar, for her patience and for letting music become a part of my daily life.

The Landmark bookstore (now sadly defunct) for housing contemporary Japanese prose.

Kala Ramesh, for her lively, participative haiku and tanka workshops.

The Instagram community of writers and poets, for the warm welcome.

Jahnavi Barua, for her poised and beautiful writing, for the conversations, for her grace, kindness and her quiet support for every Instagram post of mine.

Shachi Kale for her art and for the beautiful rendering of the cover.

The illustrators of the Instagram page @jesalwrites: Dhwani Kikani, Kalindi Suri, Sreerag Praful, Wendy Rodrigues, Vyomika Parekh, Namrata Iyer and Yuhana Syed—without their art, the page wouldn't have resonated with as many people as it does today. For their quick understanding of the spirit of the poem and for the astonishment I'd feel when their exuberant, youthful art gave a new perspective to a poem.

Curtis Key, for loving this manuscript. The enthusiasm was palpable in the first Zoom call. For being generous in creating a space where I could shape this book the way I wanted, with no restrictions. For being a delight to work with!

Priya Doraswamy for seeing something of merit in the manuscript that I'd sent her. Before the 'platform', when these were words on paper. For the brilliant advice to take to Instagram—my writing world opened up in a way that I'd never imagined. For her efforts and faith in the manuscript.

My readers, for opening their hearts and allowing my words to touch them. For writing in, asking questions, sharing their thoughts, stories, appreciation and most of all: for their abiding affection.

To my help at home – Savita Mhaske, Prajakta Pathare and Aunty, without whom this book would've taken about two more lifetimes to happen, if at all.

And friends who helped me in so many ways—you know who you are!

My mother in law Beena Kanani, for her unflagging enthusiasm for my writing.

My parents who made me feel early on, what I think, say, write—matters! My late father Kishor Malia, for doing anything and every little thing with love and affection; for seeing me always with rose-tinted glasses—more than what I was—for supporting my decision to write full-time, for things that are impossible to fit in this section, I won't try! And my mother, Harshida Malia for her sensitivity in perceiving the world and people around her, for her love for nature and peace, some of it must've trickled down to me. My brother Pratik Malia, for thinking my writing is cool! My cousin Maitri Malia, for her unstinting love for my writing.

My children, Mihika Kanani and Samika Kanani, for pushing me into a room, shutting the door, and saying from the other side, "Now write!" For taking such great care of themselves and for knowing when to stay out of each other's way, while I was doing what they had commanded me to do!

Mumma, loves you.

Spouse extraordinaire, first reader forever, Harin Kanani, for everything that you are, you inspire me. For seeing in my writing what I took many years to see.

I love you.

I. Tanpura's Strum

at the poetry reading
        you and I
                listening to
                        the same words

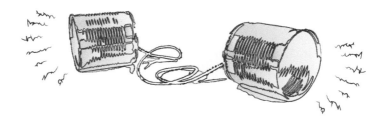

late Sunday mornings —
quiet happiness
fills me
watching you asleep

silent unlit
the phone stays —
so many Friday nights
were mine

hour of the setting moon
from lovers we
    wane into friends

you with your hurt
on one end
        me with mine
        on the other
look longingly
at the bridge between us

a tanpura's
constant strum
—you
on my mind

Jesal

how many
casualties
in 'staying true to oneself'

your mind
already at work
I stop you
with an invite
for breakfast

peeling garlic
I think of your
gentle pulling away
once I showed
you my core

soul dead mall
I'd rather use
old things
all my life

in every
orgasm with new lover
the wound
wells up fresh —
we're no longer together

gazing silently
at paragliders in Pokhara
each of us wonder
how long will we last

sensitive
like touch-me-nots
after break up

holiday mornings
long enough
to tell one another
of last night's dreams

wilted
like a bunch of flowers
held close to heart —
your promises
after break up

10 P.M. —
watching your
unwavering online status
I wait as if
outside a pleasure room

remembering
you once saying
the ex sang like Celine Dion
I skip the song
mid-play

setting sun…
you can't help
      being you
I can't stop
      being me

sixth night
you haven't called
the silence
now mocks even
my home-grown coriander

Dassera morning
balanced on the ladder
you suspend strings
of rising suns—
marigolds

4 A.M.,
wide awake
I reach out
to ruffle a sleepy you

night of
Anant Chaturdashi—
as item songs shriek
I turn away to gaze
at the quiet full moon

Ghatkopar street storefronts —
looking for lingerie
you will like

gym closed
last Wednesday of month,
   sixty
more minutes
to talk with you

us
together again
same,
and not the same

moonlit path
shimmering on sea —
will you ever return?

spring in step today,
last night
I've been loved

Lonavala skies —
flour dusted with stars
how easily
life's troubles
fall away

within our first kiss
move the foetal avatars
of all that
we will grow to be

leaving it to time
to reveal
what your intentions are,
I put away thinking much
this summer night

"Goodnight", you say
will the earth to spin faster
to wish you good morning
right away

enjoy
    listening to you talk
        as coffee percolates
            drop by drop
                between us

thunder tantrums
even the last rain
doesn't want to leave you

change
profile picture on phone
as Spring's buds
put on their
best colours

back from vacation
he in his room,
I in mine

when my pauses
speak to you —
you've got me

what's that
gentle pressure?
turn and see —
your knee resting
on mine

it's a leash —
no
you say
it's just a nudge
— I want to believe you

we've said our goodbyes
    but it's dawn
in the garden and
I walk barefoot
on dew-tipped grass

rattled by
approaching trains
I wait for you
at Ghatkopar station
a hammering heart keeping time

II. Of Kadipatta Leaves and Everything in Between

raindrops…
I wake up to
bejeweled windows

flip over
my Gucci bag
as I check aunt
into a
subsidized hospital

the pressure cooker
hesitantly
clearing its throat
before working up the nerve
to sing freely

21

obedient flour bags
sit waiting
at the chakkiwallah

how to forget you —
   this puzzle
   I've been trying to solve
   since the Palash
   put out its hardy flowers

Winter afternoon —
it alights on my heart
opening its wings
a sudden nameless happiness

kids in raincoats—
      specks of colour
in my monochrome life

sex, without the nutrient-rich
emotional soil
    I wither
like the houseplants
of someone on a holiday

                              semester end…
                              us together
                              side by side
                              even if only on
                              the student roster

hot chocolate spoon
lucky aren't you
—to jump from
an empty to a full jar

May sun
brightness that stays
even after closing my eyes

thinking
of what we were
I snap
a cinnamon stick
in two

cryogenic memories
I defrost
this winter night
to search
for the cold poetry in them

thyroid, slip disc
scars of
wives, mothers who
cared too much

walking down
childhood street
come aware
of how much
happiness I've lost

agarbatti —
a song of smoke

graceful dhoop—
    knows to fall only within
        its place

back from
Gavdevi market
        me —
the reigning queen of
fruits and vegetables

Twilight…
as mother talks of the past
my pinafore
with applique strawberries
close enough to touch

tadka burning,
old neighbour rushes in
to pluck at
Mum's kadipatta sapling

Autumn evening —
the slow swirl
of a falling leaf

was I
just a passing bee
that you let buzz
in your garden
on a solitary summer night?

off-course
even when navigated
wayward shopping cart

foreign trip—
constant this feeling
I'm in someone else's
drawing room

Spring night—
keeping my peace
at core
I exit this
combative WhatsApp group

pleading with myself
to forget past squabbles
I stand at the corner shop
as lilies for m-i-l
get wrapped up

absorbed by his hands
on the steering wheel
desire swells...

chill in room —
watching Everybody Loves Raymond
with mother-in-law

Amar Chitra Katha —
the grandma who
tells my children stories

soul and rebirth gifted
at the traffic junction —
Hare Krishna volunteer

can't stay angry
with my teenage niece,
her face hides
    a baby with pupils glossy
like pearls of the Tahitian Sea

thick dosa batter —
I paint
on the pan
a moon with holes

pure white Champa
still blooms
on smoggy highway dividers

come here, come here
that book of Murakami
in the cafe bookshelf says

monsoon plan —
wear skirts
till the topography
of legs
stays bare

hearing of my father's death
   my maid
gently wipes
his photo frame

crushed
between mammogram plates,
      "Thank you,"
words I have to drag out
to the radiologist

Mauritius sands —
I cup in my hands
the vast Indian Ocean
to touch
another shore back home

clutching close
the quietness
of Kabini forest
I enter
my Bombay home

Dusk —
waiting for the maid
who hasn't returned after payday

my gaze lingers on an
abandoned pail
by the hand pump...
nights and nights
of not being touched

New Year deadline —
catch the atheist me saying,
"Thank God,
December has 31 days!"

tired, break my run
a frog crosses showing off
his aerobic jumps

in print, the population
of my country —
I forget how to count

a snail carries
its home everywhere
from Mumbai to Maryland

rubbing sandalwood —
the fragrance of
Madurai temples
in my new home

close, near, further, far
surround sound
of the waking forest

                              morning of Rakshabandhan
                              in brother's home
                              miss my father's
                              old Rafi songs

continuity—
the blue guide uniform
now also my daughter's

after telling you
it's over
check the phone often

a dragonfly released
from a closed fist —
I stop keeping tab
on the give and take
in relationships

uninstalled Whatsapp
my heart still jumps
on hearing
someone else's
phone buzz

after the high tide
all that's left —
dregs of desire

setting the curd
my thoughts turn to
the gentle world
of mothers and kakis

Holi fire —
warm
the arctic corners
of this heart

that distance
married men
and women keep
from one another

on his lock screen
a knowing text
from an unknown woman
…so, it has happened

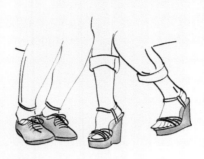

Spring evening
meeting an old friend
buried tulip bulbs
sprout

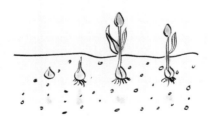

standing sprightly
at the end of the day
they delight me —
kadipatta leaves!

drawn to the kitchen
by shiny pods
of freshly peeled garlic
oh! to be so young
and new again

under the fan,
morning newspaper
yawning

Mum's home —
the pleasure of finding
salt and sugar
in the same place

kothmir sprinkled
on every dish —
    my bai
apologises

                                    last exam —
                                    doodles
                                    reappear in margins

              after exams,
              your voice
              like a slept in
              Jaipur cotton rajai

college days…
         like candy floss
disappearing on my tongue

                              all summer a mango
                              waited in its crate —
                              then turned black

on whatsapp
hmm… as in thinking
english english
hmm… as in agreeing
indian English

cry —
not so much for mother
but for my father who can't
stop missing her

broken —
she fixes herself
with filters
in selfies

a homemaker
luxuriating in the peace
of a Monday morning

the dress
at the dry cleaner's
lovelier
for not being on sale

end-stage diagnosis —
we weren't looking
when a hairline crack
emptied out
the earthen pot

gathering dusk …
Dad's diagnosis in lap
stunned
how can the laburnum
still sway gaily in the wind?

III.   Tell the Hairstylist, Keep It Long

is everything okay
he asks
as if all the blame
is mine

is everything okay
you ask
I'm too tired
to wade into these currents again

doodh ka doodh
paani ka paani
it hits me
it was sex over love

tight tee
I mine the depths
of my wardrobe
to extract
a wisp of a stole

encircled by mums
at the bus stop
I step away
to think of you

asleep
you turn away
    I still want
    your arm
    for a pillow

the gap
between pulled curtains
     us
          when we argue

inversely proportional —
the distance
you maintain
and how involved you are:
wild man

Summer night
limb-by-limb
sleep creeps in

warm clothes
just out of a dryer —
aaah! oooh!
summer happiness
in monsoon

love you
but also happy
some days
when the phone
doesn't buzz

Sunday night argument—
        even as I
                shout goodbye
part of me wants
to stay with you

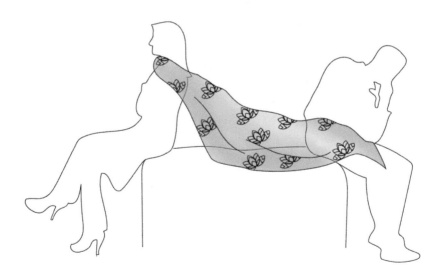

lucky girl —
your loving actions
who needs words

instant brightness!
quicker than whitening creams
when we make up

smoothing of
the jagged edges
of my heart —
when you finally call

tasting bitter
the last guava
I'd kept reserved for you

remembering in time
tell the hairstylist
keep it long
thinking someone once
said he loved long hair

after leaving
he returns
expecting
to find the same
happiness in my voice

the temple elephant's
open mouth —
my withered vagina…
a long dry Summer

on a blackboard
memories of you
I wipe off one shining letter
after another

us now —
pills taken
beyond expiry

what do you know
of waiting?
you sporadic user
of whatsapp

belly dancing
to the wind—
an empty bottle

a copperpod tree
rains flowers
indiscriminately
if you want to love,
love the world!

evening at Crossword —
reading what turns men on
in a 'feminist' magazine

abandoned by you
a d r i f t
on a warmer current
I wash up on shore

23:45
finding you online
I wonder if her hair is long

not why you left me
but *how* you
left me

seventh sleepless night —
grudge even the street dog
his afternoon nap

drive by the temple
a sense of isolation —
no goddess can save me now

how much do you like me?
65%
first class
no distinction

last sip —
love for him
peters out

broken moon —
now no longer in orbit
of your gravitational pull

unlike
the family inside
plants of my balcony
entwining limbs
around each other

brother's girlfriend over
chai christened
masala 'T'ea

monsoon's first drizzle
f l i c k e r i n g—
the yellow traffic sign

intermittent fasting…
day-by-day
I wane
like the gibbous moon

New Year's plan:
how to get you back
without having to say sorry

10th wedding anniversary—
alone in mall
would you
wink back
handsome mannequin

tabla concert—
us, cooling side by side
until the jugalbandi
begins
our argument of last night

Autumn dusk —
my grandma silent
on the window ledge

leaps my heart —
your name scrawled
on autorickshaws
stationary shops

called a hot chick
I drop the man
like something hot

IV.   First Day of Spring

on the swing
of Nani's home
my troubles sway
up and away

under the fan
a ten rupee note
inching away
on its own journey

nothing working out
I pull my fingers — snap!
this first morning of Spring

overnight
on mango trees —
blossoms arrive stealthily

Spring!
being in love
don't grudge
even the long queue
outside the voting booth

gupshup and chai with
old masis and mamis
forevergreen

m-i-l
I'm nobody's fool:
if you are nice to me
I'm nice to you

first day of Spring—
pigeon netting off
I have an avian visitor

how can I
become more lovable
no shame
in pondering this
—rainy afternoon in Shillim

waited long enough
I leave the café…
the song 'Run to you'
fading behind closed doors

31st of March —
the wonder of it
I work and work
yet have nothing
to file in tax returns

driving back
from office on Friday
free to look
at the blue sky
with nothing else on my mind!

meeting childhood friends,
years of my life
credited back

New Year morning —
deciding not to ever leave
Jesal Malia Kanani
famished and hungry,
I break this diet plan!

                    solo women —
                    feminism arrives,
                    sips and leaves
                    Starbucks

                              biting into my fifth slice
                              of pizza
                              the svelte lady
                              at the corner table
                              a receding inspiration

dupatta well-adjusted
   I order a large vodka
   on the rocks

emptying out
mum-in-law's bedpan
I age in this instant

missing
what we used to be
in the middle
of my third drink
I open Facebook

pretending to look
into the phone screen
the man in the elevator
staring at my legs

Evening at park —
all benches
taken

character on screen
sweeter
for sharing your name

a marriage lost
on the count
of his relatives
staying over hers

teaching freshmen
Aristotle's rhetorics
looking for
ethos, pathos and logos
in a Billie Eilish song

who is this imposter
impersonating a teacher
teaching them
Creative Writing

I,
who haven't found it yet
read to my students
"How To Find One's Voice"

hearing 'pastry shop'
layers of fat
accumulating in my ears

monsoon sale —
from a sea of sarees
torn
is the one I pick

car games
on Agra highway
answering
A for America

fading —
the sign saying
Restaurant Opening Shortly

the setting sun
glazes gold
a defunct petrol pump

my masi
of yesterday
nothing but
today's ashes

giving directions —
the rickshawallah
bears unnecessities
with much grace

wait a minute!
laptop screen
before blanking out

asking
when 'I' expired
this
executive renews my
gym membership

beginning to ask
when will we reach?
kids in the backseat

in midnight still
listening to his breath
rise and fall
I wonder —
> leave or stay
> leave or stay

follow my nose —
directions
to highway restrooms

pass by the cafe
where we often met —
our table
now marked
reserved

express highway—
if only the cars' speeds
matched with my life's

at the conference
dormant self-promotion genes
awaken

you say
"I lost what I desired"
I think—me too
and together
we wait for this moment to
d i s i n t e g r a t e

clamping down
her anger
the daughter-in-law
tightly clips
a pack of chips

black butterfly
descend gently
on young, green leaves

parallel lines…
we swell with love
for each other
at different times

dawn —
stationary ships
rosily glow

a lighthouse
to the toy ship that
    keeps returning
—mother on park bench

last day of March —
I'll take leave of you now
he says casually
and never returns

chill in room...
Kakaji's eyes
rest on
my backless blouse

casual invitation —
I spring back
when he instantly accepts

in the case of
Why You Don't Call Often
I identify the suspect:
ambivalence to commitment

knowing the shallowness
of a man impressed
only by appearances
I still can't help
wanting you to like me

weeping laburnum
    petals drip-drop
    under blue skies

frantic strumming
of the tanpura —
shishya's maiden performance

mother-in-law
staying over —
my home
no longer
mine

my heart
won't listen
what my mind knows
it will regret
two moons from now

a phonecall in April…
never to be celebrated
again
another anniversary

            anxious
            for the ice-cream van
            under a blazing mid-day sun

                        new tawa—
                        patterns on rotis
                        breathtakingly new

at Disneyland
   lost
with a map in hand

         try to not feel foolish
         this Midsummer day
         searching for housekeys
         yet again

                        turning forty...
                        DIY books lie
                        dusty
                        in the bookshelf

V.   Moon Face

until due date
two hearts beat
within my growing body

Fourth of May
holding a new life
in my arms
ask myself stunned
is she mine, is she mine?

acts of love
heal the healer
as much as the healed

morning song —
through the baby monitor
my baby singing to herself

rosy sky
of an early Summer dawn
she too, must've been
a young girl
before becoming my Mother

Nani's home
the smell of rajnigandha
on opening the car door

orphanage —
the cocoon
and so
the flight of a butterfly

door closing in!
on your baby fingers —
but all you see is me

Moon-face
  everyday you hide
  everyday I act surprised

sunflower —
my daughter even in sleep
keeps turning to me

first day
of playschool —
at home just me
and my baby's lonely crayons

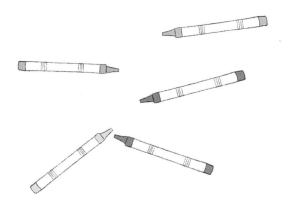

Dad away at sea
little feet
come running
to the sound
of every doorbell

12:30 PM
little feet walk in
the day is no longer
mine

summer vacation…
crossing over Dadi's threshold
wound-up toy puppy

first morning of Spring
turn my daughter's
kaleidoscope
breaking an old pattern
to set the new!

masking
the beginner's bra
with talks of flowers
in her school garden —
the first bloom of niece's
shyness before me

teenage years —
niece's fidget spinner
searching, searching
its own axis

bunny suitcase packed
angry feet
ready to leave
struggle
to turn the door lock

handmade ducky —
a child's love
rests in my palm

gypsy mother of the night
shunting between our bedroom
and the children's

losing
the holiday note
little eyes cry
thinking the holiday too
is gone

cut outs
from a toothpaste box...
time unspools
on vilambit taal
this school holiday morning

Morning —
school bags
dabba out
I sink into a sofa
that is now entirely mine

flipping through
my wedding album
offended,
baby daughter asks
where am I, where am I

summer holidays
the slow rounding
of my children's cheeks

school vacation over
time re-acquires
its neat square and rectangle shapes

daughter says
all the girls hate the boys
and all the boys hate the girls
I nod, knowing of
Time's reversals

your hand
on my breast…
daughter walks in
and from Mother Father
we turn into
Man and Woman

wanting for
me to leave
my kids
remind me
of my morning walk

hard making space
for baby Yoda
in your Star Wars collection,
when for you
I was once the universe

dessert making
with me
my daughter's enthusiasm
cools faster
than the jelly

will she feel
like a river dammed
or should I let her slip by
like a stream:
parenting...
no easy answers

if only
my daughter
could see
it doesn't matter
with my older eyes

Matheran —
the daughter I once rocked
rocks my hammock

                              end of holiday
                              folding in my blanket
                              the smell of trees

VI.   Corn Cobs at Kisama

morning mist in the rainforest
ponder on
the absurdity
that this world and mine
exist together

deforestation —
a butterfly's
slow clap

Matheran —
as I learn to relax
above my hammock
windy treetops confer
with each other

'Sprawling and Stylish'
goes the headline
a mother egret's
tired wings made to
flap a hundred miles further

corn cobs
hanging from the rooftop
at a café in Kisama
the sudden awareness of
how far I'm from home

In Japan
where everything is art
don't have
the heart to tear open
even the wrapping paper

exfoliated by
sands of Goa
now squeaky clean
inside-out

Swayambhu temple
in Kathmandu
eyes of a parent
that 'see me'
compassionately

twilight—
kaki feeding
returning parrots

in the phone booth
a sticky presence
of someone here
before me

still palms —
even they
aren't
in a vacation mood

                                    train rides on
                                    Japan rail
                                    again become a child
                                    lost in a fair

Winter —
open the window
seasons turn within
my warm room

digital detox —
every hour
I remember
to unremember
my phone

off Gateway —
only the sound of water
lapping against the
stern

clay bird
brightly painted
who do you
stand in all alert for?

Summer's
first heat waves
daydreams of mangoes
ripening in
Deogadh's cool groves

visa arriving
just in time
I hop off
to make some memories!

as I confuse
left with right
rickshawallah
misses the turn

under
my supplicating hands
p l e a s e d
the napkin dispenser
grants me three wipes

hand-knit sweater
the smell of
evening woodsmoke
in Uttarakhand

that woman
applying hand cream
nonchalantly at the Irani cafe
— I want to be!

cloudy
Himalayan afternoon
another sky
behind this sky

down this path
littered with old twigs
I walk faster
with a hammering heart

                              at dawn —
                              catch gilded fugitives
                              Himalayan peaks

déjà vu
we've spoken
of red-stemmed
amaranth leaves
under this market sun, long ago

"The point is
that we spend time together,"
you say
and continue
looking into the phone

Marve beach —
love for him
surges
retreats

his encircling flight
touches base
bated breath
finds its way back
into my ribcage

Kashmir—
everything muffled
under a blanketing rain

quiet satisfaction
spotting a Wheeler book stall
on a far-off railway station

VII.   His Body Is My Home

nestled
against me
he sleeps better
so do I

well into the day
its bitter aftertaste
tiff with a friend
this morning

"I love your words,"
he says
without hesitating
I ask,
"and me?"

Night—
you say you love me
when the world
has already
turned on its axis

in Autumn's
golden light
discover tributaries
of time
forming on my neck

why should I do
anything else
but love

year after year
the crow hatches the cuckoo's eggs
only at forty
glimmers of
understanding this Life

Evening soak —
I grope for answers
but the moving shore
of soapsuds
remains out of reach

phases 1.0-4.0
as I lull
into its lumbering
lockdown
shape-shifts

spread the jam a
little thinner —
in lockdown
learn to make
more from less

his hand on mine
the monsoon sea
surging

the peepul's
shifting leaves:
in dappled shadows
     I think,
not think of you

cloudburst —
at once
you fill all my mind

                              even as he mouths
                              my petals
                              it's you
                              that I come for

           and yet
           these thoughts of him...
           lockdown —
           discover a sunset's
           many hues

after meditation
open my eyes
a drop of rose syrup
dropped in milk
slowly swirls, spreads

Gurupurnima—
I advance
a curved gerbera
to the influencer
in my life

through the night
the hills bathed in a blue glow
of Kurinji flowers
the way I feel, when you look
at me the morning after

singing Bageshri
with thoughts of only you
I meander
and skip
meeting the sama

after gossiping
drained like a flower
in a shallow vase

knock off
the heirloom jar
setting up my new home
oh, the sweet relief
as it breaks

Spring break —
we leave the campus
with heavy baggage
and light hearts

                                        nothing more
                                        is needed
                                        his body is my home
                                        my body, his

VIII.   Grow Wild Like Kelp

Election days —
as I argue with mother
sweat the layered dhoklas
she made for me
on the coffee table

fallen copperpods
carpeting city streets
everyone
this morning
so rich!

bonsai —
I keep trimming
my desires
but all leaves tremble
only for you

pinching off the
flaky skin of a smoked brinjal
          spring away—
by its resemblance now
   to the marine world

                              in the hum
                              of the highway
                              wonder if my life
                              will count

nesting dolls—
in your stories
my story

                              houses starting
                              just at 3 crores
                              this real estate ad
                              mocks me

in a packed polythene
the purple yam
kand and papdi
chorusing together
Undhiya, Undhiya!

distant fireworks...
in my kitchen
the sound of corn popping

Jaipur block prints —
certain
past life exists
why else would I
love these

lingering long
at the gold store
not working up
the nerve to buy
"We expect you back,"
the store attendant says sternly

Summer fan
chortling away
as I gaze up
frustrated
with my stagnant life

water cut day—
spiteful tap
spitting out
spittles of water

through
the still of a summer afternoon
gliding smoothly
—a cottonseed

spoken of
but not sung
this moonless night
Bhairavi raga
loses its magic

hydra-headed thoughts...
ear-pressed
into your steady heartbeat
I find shelter
through the passage of the night

heavy flow day
all I do is
exist

on seeing
Nani's withered face
        the years
I stayed out of touch
swell like an ocean wave

running along
with my rickshaw
laughing, cavorting
Autumn's many tiny
compound leaves

shrivelling like
a touch-me-not
as diet plans
get discussed
around the table

family WhatsApp group
after I exit
the chatter
continuing long
in my head

loving myself more
turn back from the salon
and let my hair
grow wild like kelp

once again
holes in your apology
     full moon —
overlooking its contusions
I surrender to a cold brilliance

morning of Independence Day
a small paper flag
glittering on your shirt

overfamiliar guest —
I open myself
resignedly to this
river of blood
every month

after being through
the fridge's long winter
I can't expect
this pack of peas to thaw
       all
           at
               once

balcony seat
from the flyover —
the laburnums
putting on show after show
of full bloom

Summer days:
a watermelon
leans patiently
against the kitchen wall

foreseeable future —
the bend
in the flyover

Morning after —
happily place
cotyledons
of sourdough bread
facing each other

Japanese fan patterns —
daily my bai paints
the canvas of my floor

in the rickshaw
red-cheeked
as lu of April blows

tick-tock
fall copperpods
through the hourglass of
Summer

winter chill —
nipples erect
only the warm towel
to hold me in
an embrace

elaichi and mango slices
the warmth
of summer holidays
fills me

lockdown —
the desire
that I write of,
accessed only
in memories

in the Metro
speed reading
an article
on Mindfulness

can't dim
to please the in-laws
Chardham yatra —
a firefly glows
through the underbrush

m-i-l
praising her
can't shake off
this feeling of being
the other woman

construction
outside my window
how strange
to see
snot so dark

the Will
being read out
my eyes fall
on a patch in my garden
the sun overlooks

forever in a fight —
the raised curve of
this orthopaedic shoe
and my natural foot curve

after several seasons
a text from him...
desire welling up
I go
find an orange to unpeel

"You too
comeover anytime
you're in the area,"
she replies
but doesn't share her number

lockdown days
I turn off the fan
to tune in to the frequency
of the neighbours' fight

not just a tree
but also the sky
the rain
the soil
the air, the sun

angry
at being kept waiting
the heated pan
punishes
the kadipatta, at once

as if passing on
a family heirloom
Mrs. Navare
leaving her house keys
in my hands

two meals a day
I run
like a shuttle
morning-evening
between this diet plan

Evening—
with massaged limbs
I wonder
how long my masseur's
been standing on her feet

over and over
I wonder if you love me
over and over
your gestures say yes
over and over

IX. Small Talk in Office

Monday mornings
keys on office keyboards
—a fast tango

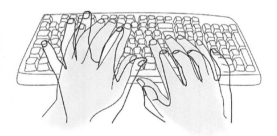

still getting used to
the office coffee
kind of new

overworked city —
Saturday evening
benches in a park
still empty

Springtime cold —
my worktable
a field
blooming with
crinkly tissue flowers

Winter solstice —
from my
office window
the sun now
on a retreating march

emerging out
of the laptop
my eyes
feast on the
street life below

beseechingly
look up to the sky
in this city
the only thing
still boundless

rising up
the toilet seat
of office
the stickiness
startling me

step out
of my cubicle
certain of
gossip trailing behind me

that lingering perfume
on entering the empty elevator
was it you?

Jaipur Hotel
sharing the
executive room
with a colleague
—pee softly

fasting day—
during lunch hour
the scrape of a spoon
against a bowl
u n b e a r a b l e

in the office cafeteria
never alone
—with my thoughts

small talk at office
until his eyes
rove over
my bare arms

wished
over and over
on Women's Day
suddenly turn
self-conscious of being a woman

Evening—
complimented even if just
on my Ikat kurta
I leave office
on a sweet note

too late!
can't stop whatsapp
from
moving on
to your status update

hoping
he won't make
anything more of it
—colleague I often chat
with at office

X. Moons of Different Planets

pilot light
after everything extinguished
some love still alive

                    through the cracks
                    of a dried-up heart
                    love peeps out — hello!
                    this hot day of April

after you leave
watch the clock shudder
yet another minute

not when it thrived
only after it's gone
I bring flowers
to our love
—everyday

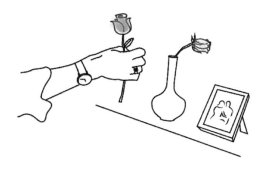

you tell me its off
I go buy myself some
fake eyelashes

I rest my foot on
your knee like a seductress
you clamp down my toes
with assumed familiarity
—just a pedicure

now that it's over
between us
involve myself in
planting buckets at home
on water-cut days

not hearing from you
I linger
on Facebook
this moonless night

promised myself to
leave if he makes me cry
one more time
— I weep on finding
myself crying

your war
with yourself
        me:
its first casualty

grateful
        to the sparrow
                who sings my sorrow away

post break-up
you post posts
that beg
to be liked

mango blossom season
unable to be tempted
into an affair
my life carries on
its usual slow pace

'Tied up today,'
he apologizes to me
and at a nearby Udupi
meets her,
his old classmate for coffee

withering away
petal-by-petal
the wild rose
in our bedroom

Spring morning—
can't deny
the lightness in my step
after break-up

peddler of fake promises
you wander about
woman-to-woman

hands of a clock–
we meet briefly
for chai and mixture
and then each
depart on our own ways

tracing letters on
sofa's velvet upholstery
—if only memories
could be erased as easily

weeks
since you buzzed
I now begin to roll up
my feelings into neat bales

Eclipse night —
relieved
my heart
finally aligned
with my mind

graceful man —
only a faint dip
in your voice
indicating
despair at rejection

after major heartbreak
   still sometimes
these seismic tremors

shyly coming out
of its shell
Spring's first
Silkcotton

moons of
different planets
now, you and I

Spring morning
forgiving everything
I click open
the chat window
but find myself unable to type

don't tell you
when you finally call
I'd perked up at
every swoosh
of an incoming text

                              reach your fb wall
                              to find
                              who is she
                              you left me for

my nipples
        your touch
                sunflowers
                        to the sun

so, "you're leaving me?"
the question I couldn't ask
time answers with
its amber silence

under winter moonlight
everything the same colour
since you left

XI. Embers of a Diwali Sparkler

Diwali days —
charcoal grays and blacks
at Zara
out of place

                              buoyant —
                              a thread pulled
                              off a faded zari kurta

khade-khade
petticoats altered
Diwali comes
early this year!

dawn lights up
blackened wicks
of yesterday's diyas

roasted besan —
smell that fills
a square room

kandil tendrils
glide quietly
in the night sky

Thanksgiving dinner —
in the distinct folds
of gujiyas
each Aunt's remembered laugh
warms this snowy night

Diwali dinner—
you with a new girlfriend
somewhere, a papad
stung by overheated oil
curls inwards

family dinner—
the chatter
of stringed Diwali lights

embers of
a Diwali sparkler
—now, you and I

XII.   Of What We Used To Be

on Whatsapp
my words to you —
neglected gray ticks

that middle aged lady
in the gym mirror
is that really me?

peepul sapling —
tonight, love bursts
through all
my self-built walls

my little
black dress
won't be bait:
do dry winds howl
through the desert of your heart?

Sita's deer —
you burst into Nallis
for that saree I want

finally
you call
but a forest of trees
grew between
Monday and Friday

Wednesday night
the phone
doesn't buzz
I slowly recoil back
into my shell

runa nu bandh
it must've been —
in the fading twilight
no clearer answer
than this

September dusk
    my knight
stoops
to massage my feet
with Odomos

after I've left —
in the silence
that prevails
the things I did for you
will speak for themselves

in evening —
birthday wishes
taste like a tea
gone cold

the path of
a yellow wagtail
'evolving'
into a woman
you will like

early April
smelling rain
can't shake off
this feeling in my bones
you will leave soon too

choosing
to look only at
the good
I drain with a fork
a mango from the pickle jar

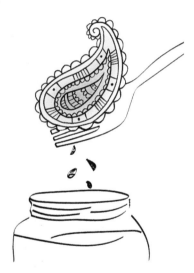

period days
stow away
the whites

Pale —
the laughter in the party
after our fight

dark Monsoon skies
even so, a jasmine bud's
slow unfurling

breathtaking
not the thunderstorm
but the young shoot
supple and hopeful
under streaks of lightning

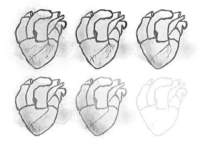

14th night
    of the waning moon
        tiring to be the man
        and woman
           of this relationship

Evening —
weary of the day
we
draw warmth
meeting again

            pull out books to arrange
            not knowing what to do
            after you left

                        in Mainland China
                        love shared
                        one by two

holding my hand
without acquiescence
I'm surprised
by the heat
my petals give away

after lunch hour
the empty tables
reserved for sparrows

by the time
you call back
bucket under tap
overflowing with love

ricocheting
in my mouth
like cold marbles
—words of truth

not knowing
if you will return
all my days enacted
over a canvas of longing

bone up
on sleep techniques
come night, watch
trees whirl on bare walls
until dawn

Election days—
I somberly exit
the family WhatsApp group

Dassera morning
wearing slippers
we weave our way
to buy strings of
marigolds

rainy July night
memories flooding
I unfollow you
on Facebook once again

you say
"Sunday I'll be working,"
quickly,
I jump in to bargain off
the Monday

if it's hurting you
as much as it's hurting me
we're still connected—
even if only
by this pain

weekday or weekend
I water
the gourd seed
knowing
it will bloom one day

city unlock...
rinsing off
with a facepack
the week's disappointments
I go out to see him

a couple —
the wayward jalebi
and the upright fafda

wearing Chanel
and eyeliner
I set off
only to the kitchen
—lockdown days

Summer's perfume —
I breathe in each day
from a cupped palm
the smell of mangoes

want to be with you
but also hear
the roar of life calling

'Spouses and lovers'
the matter-of-factness
of the title
leaves me
breathless

matrimony meet —
rides up
the neck of my silk kurta
choking me

night of Purnima
the full realisation
that you've left me

Evening —
reading aloud fairy tales
our love of
no commitments
now feels inadequate

                              find better things to do
                              says the man
                              I've loved twenty-four moons

after its over
stop matching
lingerie
by color anymore

XIII.   Words Become Play

only when
I'm not worried
about adulation or criticism
or measuring up:
words become play

                                        steep myself
                                        in books
                                        willing the words
                                        to flow

at my desk
over the roar of traffic
I write of moist fronds
and lush green moss

book deal signed
waiting in the sink
disgruntled dishes

wondering what to do
with the 'cut' sentence
I stare
at the now empty space
between lines

reading—
like waters of Ganga
poured
over
buried words

Darling,
I'll make thunderstorms
with you'
—IG poetry
frightens me

returning from the beach
with a good catch
of words

write haiku
to myself
in my head
all day

Credit to the Illustrators

Dhwani Kikani
  Graphic & UX designer | Visual storyteller
  ⊚ @dhwani_11
  pages 1, 3, 4, 5, 11, 18, 33, 34, 40, 46, 62, 64, 75, 76, 97,
  101, 167, 172, 178, 184, 187

Kalindi Malia Suri
  Graphic designer | Editorial designer
  ⊚ @kalindims
  pages 2, 6, 23, 42, 44, 52, 54, 55, 56, 57, 59, 61, 67, 68,
  70, 186, 188

Namrata Iyer
  Human centred designer | Visual storyteller
  ⊚ @itstalkingtofu
  pages 27, 185, 190

Sreerag Praful
  Communication designer | Artist
  ⊚ @holmes.draws
  pages 16, 49, 51, 105, 106, 109

Vyomika Parikh
  Illustrator | Visual experience designer
  ⊚ @vyomikaparikh
  pages 120, 156, 162, 164

Wendy Rodrigues
  Illustrator | Graphic designer
  ⊚ @wendyrodrigues__
  pages 20, 71, 79, 81, 83, 85, 95, 102, 107, 126, 127, 131,
  133, 142, 144, 169, 170, 198

About the Cover Artist

Shachi Kale is a visual storyteller, graphic designer, and children's book illustrator. Her art is a reflection of her journey through life...both the external journey, from India to Arizona, the journey through marriage and motherhood and an internal journey that takes place as she traverses new emotional landscapes. Shachi's paintings have a narrative woven into them, and her depictions of the female form are both autobiographical and universal to women grappling with their place in the world.

Shachi uses watercolors, acrylics, embroidery, and digital arts. She is fascinated by folk art from around the world, the artists' use of flat colors, simple perspective, and storytelling. She is also drawn to Indian miniature art and the patterns and decorative elements used in them. The vibrant and rich colors of her palette are a legacy of her Indian heritage, and the narrative elements are an influence from her work as a children's book illustrator.

You can also follow her explorations and journey on instagram @shachidreams, or
email her at shachidesign@gmail.com